Poems and Prayers to Ponder

Contemporary Reflections of Faith and Being

Written by J. J. Tschantz

Illustrations by Estelle J. Tschantz

Poems and Prayers to Ponder: Contemporary Reflections of Faith and Being
Copyright 2018 by J.J. Tschantz

Illustrations by Estelle J. Tschantz

This book has no gender, no face, no denomination or race.

When you read it, you may smile, laugh or cry, and also wonder—why?

Contents

Provocative

Enlightening through avenues of self-interpretation, personal awareness, and experiences

As I muddle through each day, I turn my head
    the other way.

Staring through a slimy mask, ignoring every
    single task.

Expecting others to do for me all these things
    I never see.

Feeling very weak and vain, knowing I
    must cause such pain.

Scared by what I think I see—Is that person
    really me?

My friend and I, we had a rift;
 then one day I received a gift.

A sullen dove ready to take flight
 into the darkness of the night.

A true treasure from above: a sign of hope,
 a sign of love.

Silly as it may seem, was this by chance or
 just a dream?

Embrace the moment, look to the sky, never
 question or deny.

A dove in flight I truly see, a sign of
 peace from him to me.

Those thoughts we keep to ourselves, are treasures
    we share with no one else.

Like the mist on the grass of a new dawn, or
    the feathers of a beautiful swan.

Like the words of a song that never go away, but
    play in your head all of the day.

Like the first kiss you never forget, and remember
    always when you met.

Like the tears you cried for your first lost friend—when
    will this heartache ever end?

All of these memories we covet forever, knowing we
    will forget them never.

When your heart is truly shattered, gone are
    all the things that mattered.

Trying to rebuild a life, yearning so much
    to end the strife.

Feeling lost and all alone, having no one
    to call your own.

Losing all your self-control, hurting beyond the
    depths of your soul.

Planning not so far ahead, facing life with a
    feeling of constant dread.

Believing this too will pass, knowing all you
    need to do is ask.

Finally able to see the light, face the fears,
    and not the flight.

There's a sadness within that continues to grow. How
will I stop it? I do not know.

An empty feeling to leave behind, replacing it with a
kindness I hope to find.

Searching forever for a cure, never progressing—
why am I so insecure?

Feeling that I'm not alone, but always responding like
a wasted drone.

Needing to find what I'm looking for before I leave
and shut the door.

Time is hardly on my side. I'm afraid this life is just
a wasted ride.

Why can't you open the next door? Why are you
    so afraid to explore?

Search your heart for what you need; put
    aside your nasty greed.

Pride can ruin all that's good; are you doing
    all you could?

Planning just to mend your ways will not promise
    better days.

Change is something you must try—not to worry
    or ask why.

Faith is the power you must feel so your
    heart can finally heal.

Will I be when I am not? Will I think and
    still have thought?

Could I still see with my eyes, or are
    they now a pair of spies?

Will time be all that remains, or does it
    evaporate like the rains?

Should I ever feel a touch, or is that
    expecting way too much?

Do I have feelings, or, just numb, will I be
    willing to succumb?

Answers someday I may know when it's
    time for me to go.

Stories we will never hear of the memories
    they held so dear.

Trying to forget and never tell that
    they did it very well.

Feeling sad but oh so brave, regretting the lives
    they could not save.

Lonely hours all alone, when they hear, shots in
    the distance in their ear.

Echoes of the sounds of war, bouncing off Earth's
    molten core.

Missing those who were left behind, seeing them
    always in their mind.

Reoccur, Reoccur, Reoccur: Life is nothing
    but a constant blur.

On a treadmill every day, plodding along but
    never on your way.

Have the initiative to make a plan; accept the
    challenge, you know you can!

Find a new path, then spread your wings; open
    the door to many new things.

When your dreams are in your sight, write off
    the past and bury the fright.

Always trust in who you are, but never be
    afraid to reach too far.

I stopped by to see a friend one day, to find his
feelings had gone astray.

No longer listening to what I thought and never
caring what I sought.

Turning but his cheek to me, ignoring all that
I hoped it could be.

Wishing I were very wrong, trying hard
to be so strong.

Seeking hard to make amends, hating that this
would be how it ends.

Trying hard to clear my head, but melting
slowly inside instead.

Forcing myself to walk away, but wishing so
that I could stay.

Feeling my heart begin to shred, scared so much
of what lies ahead.

Dreading to ever be alone, hating the thought of
the unknown.

Thoughts are things we think each day, but often
    are afraid to say.

Swirling in our heads like leaves, slowly falling
    from the trees.

Forcing us to stop and think: Is there something
    on the brink?

Is it getting close and near, and when will it
    ever disappear?

Now the courage pounds in our ears, gently
    silencing all the fears.

Able to focus through new eyes, seeing clearly
    where the future lies.

The tragedy of a life left behind as I
    slowly lose my mind.

Thinking of what should have been, never
    happened now or then.

Wishing for a second chance, not ever getting
    that extra dance.

Hoping this is all in my dreams, hearing loudly
    my virtual screams.

Trying to soothe a broken heart: What do I
    do? How do I start?

Wanting always to try again; when will these
    feelings ever end?

Things will never be what they should have been; will I feel better? If so, when?

When will my broken heart ever heal? How can this catastrophe truly be real?

Feeling worse than ever before, constantly praying that there will be no more.

Hearing things that cannot be, wondering if it's really happening to me.

Knowing nothing will ever be the same, wishing this were just a game.

Hearts are broken, forever scarred, fearful a new way of life will be extremely hard.

I see a creature in the field—will he
    strike or will he yield?

Looking always for his prey, so they won't
    see another day.

Frightened so of the unknown, wishing
    they were not alone.

Seeing nothing from behind, behaving exactly
    as if they were blind.

Thrashing ahead with mortal fear, knowing
    for sure the end is near.

Do you see a parallel that they, unfortunately,
    will not live to tell?

When fear always leads the way, the stalker never
    goes away.

Sometimes it's hard to start the day with a hole
in your heart that won't go away.

Like a vault in your soul that continues to grow,
blocking your path each way you go.

Trying forever to leave where you've been, afraid
to learn how to start again.

Needing the courage to walk away, or for all of
eternity this feeling will stay.

Now voiding yourself of this terrible dread, next
clearing your body and your head.

Finally realizing how great it will be to, at last, be
able to set yourself free.

Watching the ashes float to the curb—this place
 is nothing but a charred blurb.

On the threshold of a new life, such a sorrowful
 and pitiful sight.

All the treasures of the past becoming memories
 that will never last.

Only a little speck in time, disappearing slowly, as
 we cross the line.

Where do we go from here? The reality of it
 all is so unclear.

When will anything ever matter? Is this all nonsense
 and idle chatter?

Could there really be a new start? Such a gesture
 comes only from the heart.

Do we want to take a break, looking at life
    as some big mistake?

Do we lie, or do we tell? Are we
    quiet, or do we yell?

Do we ever plan ahead, or do we always
    scramble instead?

Do we make much ado, or is it constantly
    something new?

Do we brake at every turn? When are we
    ever going to learn?

Is this real or in my head, drowning out
    the constant dread?

Happy is not a way of life; for me, the fun
    is in the strife.

Why do I cry? I do not know. How can
my heart hurt me so?

Wishing my pain would go away: why I'm
sad, I cannot say.

Wiping the tears from my face, hoping they
won't leave a trace.

Hiding all my grief inside, trying to protect
my selfish pride.

Hoping the truth will be heard; afraid to say
a single word.

Of Faith

*Inspiring exploration, recognition, renewal, and
possible confirmation of faith*

Of Faith

Oh, behold the mighty sea in its
    zealous revelry!

But listen and you will hear its quiet
    wisdom, oh so clear.

All so massive in its scope,
    reverberating signs of hope.

Such a gift from heaven above, a symbol of
    His eternal love.

When you're sad and feeling down, just like
you've been knocked around,

It's time to stop and search your soul, looking
for a brand-new goal.

Trying hard to change your path, ready now
to face the wrath.

Seeking guidance you might fear, then knowing
finally He is near.

Of Faith

Please don't let these stories go untold—shout
them loud and oh so bold.

All the lies that people want to hear, let them be
received loud and clear.

Then our souls will be set free, as we collect the
message right from Thee.

Knowledge of the truth will ring, so open up your
hearts and sing.

As I'm standing in the sand, it would be
the only land.

Water as far as I can see, the only person
being me.

Nothing else do I hear but the sound of the
surf in my ear.

Knowing I am all alone, trying not to
scream or moan.

Feeling yet so close to Thee, as my heart pounds
hard in me.

Seeing not a boat in sight fills my being all
with fright.

Hoping not that this could be, searching the heavens
all for Thee.

Is this all just a dream? Should I cry, or do I stop
to wonder why?

Knowing not to give up hope, but this is life: always
a slippery slope.

Of Faith

Hide your fears: put on a smile as you're
    shaking all the while.

Knowing you will do your best, planning to
    pass every test.

Looking forward, never back, always trying
    to stay on track.

Feeling a sadness you cannot bear, hoping
    for peace and not despair.

Reaching to the skies above, praying for His
    unconditional love.

Innocence is what we first know, slipping
away as we grow.

Looking for a place of peace, hoping it is
within our reach.

Trying hard to balance our day, learning that
we need to pray.

Trusting in the Lord above, wanting to be
worthy of His love.

Gratified to our core: knowing now, we need
nothing more.

Of Faith

Looking for answers that will never be—only
    if I look to Thee.

Wanting not to be the same, trying hard to
    face the shame.

Fearing what is the unknown, scared to ever
    be alone.

With a heart that is so shattered, forgetting all
    that really mattered.

Wishing I would have a plan—nothing special,
    nothing grand.

Knowing it is not too late, but leaving nothing
    up to fate.

Trying to create something fine with the future
    on the line.

Throwing away this terrible shroud; then, at last,
    I can be proud.

See the raindrops on the door, slowly dropping
to the floor?

Hear the thunder from the sky? Is God angry?
Does He cry?

He is saddened, I must say, when He sees you
look away.

Finding good in all you do, wishing He could
follow you.

Always watching from above, showering you
with unconditional love.

Of Faith

Walking down the street one day, I saw a man
    who stopped to pray.

Feeling not ashamed at all, just like he
    had made a call.

With a faith that would not waiver, such a feeling
    one would savor.

Seeing life for all it's worth, each new day we
    have on Earth.

As you start each new day—never, ever
   forget to pray.

Pray for those on Earth you love and for those
   in heaven above.

Thank Him for the blessings you receive; all you
   need is to believe.

He will help to shift your load as you travel each
   new road.

Of Faith

Why does the sea get so mad with waves so
　　strong? Is God so sad?

Watching us from heaven above, His heart
　　swelling with unbridled love.

Are we listening with deaf ears? Here comes the
　　rain. Are those His tears?

Do we need to mend our ways, pray for happiness
　　and better days?

See the sun, then know it's true: God wants only
　　the best for you.

As I walk through each new door, I
    feel uneasy to my core.

Being strong and brave, I try; but I
    have fear—I cannot lie.

Always scared of the unknown, so hoping
    that I'm not alone.

Seeking strength from heaven above, praying
    for His eternal love.

Will He ever let me down? Not if my faith
    remains my crown.

Of Faith

Heard a song of wondering fear; oh so
confident He is near.

Guiding us in every way, walking us through
each new day.

Knowing that it is a must that we never lose
our trust.

Crawling down a hill to see if He will still
follow me.

Trying hard to move ahead, only marking
steps instead.

Learning how to trust in Thee may be the thing
that sets me free.

Each night when I go to bed, all my prayers
　　are in my head.

Can He read my thinking mind? Will He know
　　they're sweet and kind?

If I do not use my voice, will He know that
　　is my choice?

Then I'll ask for forgiveness and love, and His
　　guidance from above.

Of Faith

Such a small creature do I see: a creation from
God, just for me.

Why do I fear such a small being? Have I no faith
in what I'm seeing?

Strong and mighty to the core; that's why He
created more.

When we're very far from home, are we really
all alone?

Do our memories ease the fear that our family
is not near?

Trying now to search our soul, looking for a
different role;

Then we hear a voice from within, telling us
we too can win.

Feeling now we can move ahead without the
fear or the dread.

Knowing there's a strength from above, guided
by His undying love.

Of Faith

I'm so sorry for the bad thoughts I had today. I
    just wish they would go away.

Searching for a kindness instead may begin to
    brighten days ahead.

With a perpetual frown on my face, not ever able
    to keep up the pace.

Praying for help from above, hoping to be worthy
    of His unconditional love.

This may be a valid start, but only if the feelings
    are sincerely from the heart.

Do we linger? Do we stray? Do we want
    to run away?

Are we fearful? Are we sad? Do we know
    good from bad?

Seeking answers from above, praying for
    His eternal love.

This is not a hopeless task; all you need
    to do is ask.

Of Faith

As I lay me down to sleep, my heart always
skips a beat.

Knowing the day is at an end, hoping He will
be my friend.

Thanking Him for all His love and the miracles
from above.

Sharing on the earth each day all of His blessings
in every way.

Appreciating Him for all He gives; praising Him for
all that lives.

Trusting Him to guide my way, knowing He won't
promise another day.

Help me, Lord, with each new day; do not let
me go astray.

Hear my prayers and know I'm true—faithful
as I trust in You.

Make me aware and full of hope; help me learn
how to cope.

Trust that fear will make me strong,
separating right from wrong.

Truth is love. That's my belief, as faith is always
my relief.

Of Faith

Simplicity

Easy reading and insightful meaning

Simplicity

Hear the surf hit the shore, steadily drumming
forevermore.

See the white foam dot the sand as the water
hits the land.

As the puff balls disappear, see the sand so
soft and clear.

This constant cleansing is not a test; the amazing
ocean never rests.

Ring! Ring! Ring! Hear the bell sing!
    For a life that is no more, like a song
    without a score.

Memories are fading fast, becoming
    soon part of the past.

Trying hard to save the day, as we watch
    it slowly slip away.

Just a spot in all that's grand, like
    the ocean's grain of sand.

Simplicity

I cry for what should have been, wishing
    I could try again.

Someone selfish has taken that away, hoping
    to have a better day.

Never looking past the now, sadly
    forgetting about the how.

Thinking of myself, you see—that is what is
    wrong with me.

Things may never be the same—this life is
    not a child's game.

Leave the past and look ahead; find
    the passion, stomp the dread.

Trust in all you want to be; make a plan
    that sets you free.

Never falter, have no fear; renew your faith
    and keep it near.

Simplicity

Will you help me—will you please—to be
    calm and more at ease?

To clear the thumping from my head, and the
    thoughts of constant dread.

Maybe a smile could be a start, making me
    feel warm at heart.

Knowing I could have a friend may put these
    feelings to an end.

When in doubt, count me out; you don't have
    to scream or shout.

You don't need to ring a bell; you don't
    need to cry or yell.

You just need to stand your ground and be a leader
    all around.

Silence is the loudest sound—nothing ever is
    more profound.

Simplicity

Never will we leave behind all that's
  growing in our mind.

Not to worry about the space; there will
  always be a place.

Having wisdom is not cheap, but definitely
  something we will reap.

Like the dawn of each new day, learning
  never goes away.

If you are ready to settle for less, life could
    be a total mess:

Never going where you could, never being
    who you should.

Dissatisfied with each new day, unable to ever
    find your way.

Better things will never come, if you're willing
    to succumb.

Blaming others for your demise; always hiding
    behind a disguise.

"Coping," a word I do not know—sadness
the only emotion I can show.

Trying hard to bury the past, searching for a
future that may not last.

Reaching out for better things, never afraid
to spread my wings.

Seeing life for all it's worth, embracing each
new day here on Earth.

How do we see others through our eyes: as equals
or in disguise?

Feeling we are better than they, keeps the bonding
far at bay.

If we are to cross the line, we must learn how to
redefine—

Seeking answers to all that's false, or this could be
a total loss.

Wanting the truth to be heard, but never saying a
single word.

Simplicity

Yes, I had a thought today that would
    never go away—

Always replaying in my head, just like
    jumping on the bed.

Wishing it were in my dreams; nothing
    is ever as it seems.

Hoping it would disappear, a constant
    echo in my ear.

A horrible way to start the day, but now
    it's time to run the play.

Just some thoughts before I go—
    things to ponder, things to know.

Time to listen, time to hear, always with
    an open ear.

Trying to preserve a friend, seeking
    judgment to the end.

Having but an open heart is the only
    way to start.

Simplicity

There are things I would rather not see—kinks in the
armor all around me.

Words of wisdom I need to hear; when my
faith I doubt, I fear.

Letting others guide the way will lead to roads that
go astray.

Being strong may raise some doubt, but strength and
spirit are the only route.

When I'm tired, I go to bed, where I rest
my weary head.

Things are changing every day, but I will
never run away.

Let's face the music and do the dance; it
may be my only chance.

Live life and be free, because there is just
one of me.

Simplicity

Projections of the future—do we succumb,
    afraid to live in the past? It's so humdrum.

New things are scary, this is true, but playing it safe is
    a waste of time for you.

Shedding your skin, not afraid to see the light, takes away
    the fear and eliminates the fright.

Being bold may be the only way, to look ahead, not back,
    and create a brand-new day.

I see the forest, but where are
the trees?

They're standing tall and stately,
blowing in the breeze.

A quiet haven for animals to rest—
nature at its very best.

Simplicity

Trying to overcome a fear, never listening
    but trying to hear.

Knowing time is running out—afraid to look
    or turn about.

Like running a race without a start, realizing
    it's only in my heart.

Wishing this were not for real; wanting to be
    on an even keel.

Leaving all the bad behind, searching
    for the good to find.

We make mistakes, but we can change once we
   begin to magnify our range.

To see ourselves for all we're worth: to fortify our
   hearts with our rebirth.

To scale the mountains, to skim the seas, to fall
   down on bended knees,

Discovering the road ahead is clear, just waiting
   now for us to steer.

Simplicity

Thoughts are things inside my head that keep me
   awake when I go to bed.

Things to forget about my day, memories I wish
   would go away.

Closing my eyes so I can rest, but always
   failing to pass that test.

Simple is the way to go, each and
    every day, you know.

Once you've tried all the rest, simple
    is the very best.

Simplicity

Let's be nice my mother said; remove all the
  nasties from your head.

Do unto others as you would be—a friend to
  all, as you would see.

Always look for better things; never be afraid
  to spread your wings.

Have hope for each new day—feel the power
  in every way.

Be careful not to run, or you may miss all
  of the fun.

Age should have no boundaries on your life, cultivating
your potential to help conquer the strife.

As you travel down the road for many miles, time never
lets you forget all the beautiful smiles.

Patience radiates steadily from your soul, allowing
you to accept every challenge and new role.

Possibilities present themselves everyday; experience
helps you choose the game to play.

Never fearing that which you don't know—understanding
always that there's time to grow.

Moving forward with increasing speed, not afraid and
forever planning, to take the lead.

Simplicity

About the Author

J.J. Tschantz is a retired public school speech pathologist with over thirty years of experience. She received her bachelor of science degree from Florida State University and her master of education degree from Kent State University. During the midst of her career, she wrote a foundation grant and received funding to open a private preschool for children with learning disabilities and handicaps called Sights on Success. She is married and has three children and seven grandchildren.

You may contact the author at jjtschantz@gmail.com.

CPSIA information can be obtained
at www.ICGtesting.com
Printed in the USA
FFHW020654071218
49788034-54276FF